Psychological Perspective of Organizational Goal Setting through Valuable Framework of Emotions

Psychological Perspective of Organizational Goal Setting through Valuable Framework of Emotions

Dr. Nidhi Kaushal

CWP

Central West Publishing

Disclaimer
Every effort has been made by the publisher and author while preparing this book, however, no warranties are made regarding the accuracy and completeness of the content. The publisher and author disclaim without any limitation all warranties as well as any implied warranties about sales, along with fitness of the content for a particular purpose. Citation of any website and other information sources does not mean any endorsement from the publisher and author. For ascertaining the suitability of the contents contained herein for a particular lab or commercial use, consultation with the subject expert is needed. In addition, while using the information and methods contained herein, the practitioners and researchers need to be mindful for their own safety, along with the safety of others, including the professional parties and premises for whom they have professional responsibility. To the fullest extent of law, the publisher and author are not liable in all circumstances (special, incidental, and consequential) for any injury and/or damage to persons and property, along with any potential loss of profit and other commercial damages due to the use of any methods, products, guidelines, procedures contained in the material herein.

A catalogue record for this book is available from the National Library of Australia

NATIONAL LIBRARY OF AUSTRALIA

ISBN (print): 978-1-922617-08-8

About the Author

Dr. Nidhi Kaushal is a Ph.D. holder in Management Studies from the Indian Institute of Technology, Roorkee. She holds a master's degree in Business Administration and a bachelor's degree in Computer Science from Kurukshetra University, India as well. She has been interested and indulged in research works related to Entrepreneurship, Leadership, Wisdom Literature, Management, and Indigenous Studies. During her Ph.D., she has identified the indigenous studies of literature and folklore related to Leadership and Management and presented her work in various international conferences and research publications across the globe. Working as a researcher, she is exploring Leadership with the study of Creative writings and ancient Indian scriptures, and this is her contribution to the academic research.

Preface

Emotions are central psychological forces of an individual, which relate his inner personality with the outside environment and reflect his behavior during organizational functioning, because any task performed with integrity and optimism generates pleasing results, while any activity done with a cumbersome and miserable state gives lesser outcomes. In the ancient period, *Rasa-paddhati* have been used to analyze people's psychological expressions and their personality attributes, like the act of valor of a person shows his quality of bravery, which introduces his personality of *Veer-rasa*. It is the traditional ancient Indian emotional mechanism that enlightens the classical form of new behavioral concepts. Aesthetic rasas specifically represent the preformed structure of the human mind and its positive expressions. They are not the only demeanor of expression, but also the real and sustaining form of emotions and exhibit their vitality in tales or melodies. Consequently, folklore acts as a medium to learn various contexts of people's emotional aspect and their effect on the life transformation process, because tales glorify the attributional strength of their characters through the central theme and their approach for achieving the target. An individual's state of mind and sentiments have a direct relation with the execution of the work and their emotional impact influences the goal-setting process of the organization and its realization as well. However, the modern psychological methods of learning the emotional pattern of an organizational leader have their implications in the present era, but the classic methods have their uniqueness and equivalent relevance in identifying his expressions as well.

Through the ancient context of *rasas*, this work enriches the contemporary ideology of emotional framework, and also signifies the impact of sentiments on the leader's performance, during the organizational task of goal setting. It includes a theoretical framework of emotions with the concept of examining the leader's approach and behavior, which recognizes the influential role of virtues, and their psychological effects on ethical goals. For potential research in the related fields of Leadership and Organization, it is an effort of intriguing study with an emphasis to provide an insight into the primordial notion of emotions.

Abstract

Goal setting is an essential strategic process of organizational development, which incorporates personality attributes such as coordination, harmony, endurance, knowledge, self-control, and empathy for its successful execution. A leader's cohesion with emotions is very important while developing policies because the intensity of his emotional potential has a profound effect on planning and execution, which also provides him an outlook of their positive or negative prospects. In ancient Indian cultural texts, the irony of the human's emotional mechanism has been explained by ancient scholars through the *Rasa-Siddhanta*, whereas the need and importance of the goals have propounded through folklore. These practices have identified human emotional behavior and its significance to set the objective, and this chapter has analyzed the pre-eminence and viability of purpose in human life through these aspects and presents a diverse perspective to understand the concept of a goal. This literary work develops a novel theory that would address the role of emotions in goal setting in an organizational environment.

Introduction

Blair (2003) observes that a goal is a specific, measurable accomplishment to be achieved within a specific time frame and there is a self-generated or pre-existing but ever-evolving mixture of differing and frequently divergent goals in organizations (Schnelle, 2008). The theory of goal-directed action postulates that in every action, two classes of changes function, such that adaptational and constructional. The first one refers to the external changes after an action that provides a different situation for further actions, and the second one is related to internal changes of the person, group, or organization (Valach & Wald, 2002). Goal setting culminates in the formation of a goal intention, which expresses a commitment to achieve the chosen goal (Bagozzi et al., 2003). It is one of the most effective ways, to achieve successful behavioral change (Barlow et al., 2010), and involves establishing a delicate balance between planning and improvisation (Blair, 2003). The focus of the goal-setting theory is on the core properties of an effective goal (Locke & Latham, 2002), and the influential practice of goal setting is the initialization of our efforts, which helps to decide the objective of our life. The goal is the essence of all that we think of what it means to be human (Moskowitz & Grant, 2009), and it plays an analogous role in the explanation of human behavior (Slade, 2013). The goal process has maintained through the operation of a positive discrepant feedback loop (Fujita & MacGregor, 2012), while emotional regulation involves cognitive restructuring, tolerance, and behavioral changes (Leahy et al., 2011). Emotional motivation has required in the goal setting and to devise, plan, and execute corresponding actions (Frijda, 2004).

Organizational goal setting is an important exercise, which includes analyzing all the related aspects concerned with it. It is not an instant decision-making process but an intensive churning, which has emphasized the associated actions and their consequences. It is a perceived and composite task of the organization's practice, and sensible judgment performed with a cautious and thoughtful approach provides profitable outcomes. The process of organizational goal setting is similar to defining the purpose of an individual's life. An engaging target works like a magnetic force, which motivates employees to perform with their full efficiency, which helps in the development of their skills consequently, the psychological aspect of the goal has a prominent role in defining the organization's model. Goal-oriented activities are the means of honoring life in which human personality is developed by enduring the pain of struggle, and the actions of an organization equally affect all the factors involved. This Chapter has elaborated the role of emotional perspective in organizational goal-setting, which has categorized into five parts such as (1) Inference of Goal-Setting as Dynamic Obligation of the Organization; (2) The Ancient Concept of Emotions like *Rasa-Siddhanta* and its Pertinence in Goal-Setting; (3) The Consequences of Ethical Goals and their Influence in Developing Human Character; (4) Recognizing the Notion of Goals and Effectiveness of a Positive Mind-Set through Tales; (5) An interpretation of significant *Rasas* required for goal accomplishment.

Inference of Goal Setting as Dynamic Obligation of Organizations

Goals are the inherent part of our personal and professional lives, which always keep us active and alive, and provide true meaning and a prime reason for our existence in the social world. Cavallo and Fitzsimons (2012) find that manging individual goals and social goals is a common and essential part of daily life, and inter-goal dynamics often play a role in determining the progress that has made toward each goal. In developing the role of purposes and priorities in decision making, goals have viewed not as atomic entities, but as composite objects with a defined structure (Slade, 2013). The precepts of the goals include that they should guarantee congruency with your life purpose, provides happiness on accomplishments, and if not, then there is a need to comprehend your motives (Daniels, 2013). People engaged in valued activities for their own sake because they derive pleasure, satisfaction, and some other valued benefit from doing so (Brophy, 2008). Goals for every individual have coordinated with overall organizational objective and strategy (Griffin & Moorhead, 2011), and a manager has particularly concerned with setting objectives and goals, developing plans, strategies, policies, making job assignments, coordinating, and controlling (Agarwal, 1982). Organizational optimization establishes that framework within the organization in a quicker and more synchronized way to ensure that the probability of success to the leader with reigns (Hutcherson, 2014). Goals are related to affect in that areas set the primary standard for self-satisfaction with performance (Locke & Latham, 2006). High level strategic organizational objectives determine the lower-level objectives and strategies that cascade down throughout the rest of the organization (Hutcherson, 2014).

The effectiveness and productivity of any organization have based on its overall objective, and practices, and procedures related to it. The goal of any organization, point towards a desired state or condition that has not yet accomplished (Gamage, 2006), and A plan identifies the tasks required to accomplish the goal by employees (Dobson & Wilson, 2008). Organizational effectiveness is a vector that includes quantifiable and non-quantifiable outputs and reflects the quality and the relationships of outputs to broad organizational goals and objectives (Jain et al., 1997), and organizational goals are much woven into the very fabric of an organization, superseding individual goals (Berger & Brownwell, 2012). The P's of organizational goals are products, processes, patronage, people, performance, and profits (Blair, 2003). Alignment helps everything to work together properly and in synchronization, and organizational alignment is the key to optimizing the execution of organizational strategy. It maximizes the efforts within the organization (Hutcherson, 2014). The accomplishment of an objective does not define the completion of entire organizational work, but after that, organizations shift their attention to new goals and, this system indicates that goal setting is an on-going process (Kirst-Ashman, 2007).

Strong mental states and positive attitude makes a target possible and gives the strength to the individual to attain the desired objective. Motivation and commitment are important for behavioral change in the individuals (Barlow et al., 2010). People are emotionally connected to their goal when they can see, and feel their goal, when it is necessary to their survival and test their limits (Murphy, 2010). The more emotion that is attached to a goal, the stronger the drive is within an individual to accomplish that goal (Rohn, 2011). Emotions constitute the most tangible and fundamental attitude in the quest for the sacred and self-discovery by humans (Bilimoria & Wenta, 2015), and they are always and necessarily linked to behavior or, at least, to changes in behavioral readiness (Frijda, 1996). Aspirations help us to find meaning through a sense of purpose, which is something larger than ourselves (Shapiro, 2010). Goals have a vital aspect and role in transforming the present conditions of an individual and for improving his personality by engaging in the humane efforts related to his work. An instance representing the prominence of goal in a person and its role in the development has been given below:

Once, Abraham Lincoln worked as a laborer in the fields so as to earn money during his young days so that he could meet his daily needs. He wanted to buy some books to read, so he worked hard continuously. With his great effort, he bought the books finally, and read it with full enthusiasm.

One day, his master asked him that if he was fond of studying, then why he worked as a laborer? He said that he would not always indulge in hard-working activities because all these were only for some duration or until he fulfilled his needs.

Then, he asked, what do you want to be? He said that he would become president one day. He will study hard and prepared himself as a leader and will get a chance for this. And finally, his steadfastness in achieving the goal brought that golden opportunity in his life, and he became the President of America. He attained a powerful position in the world because he already set his goal earlier in his life (Vaswani, 2015). This story shows that an individual's goals represent the tasks and direction of life and drive him to achieve them.

Some aims of life have set during the adolescence period by individuals, which have shown the path of success throughout until they remain attainable, and they have targeted all their actions and efforts toward those goals and affirmed to get them. This story has a wonderful lesson and implication of goal setting in one's life, which reflects the qualities such as, strong determination, brainpower, caliber, and rational efforts as well as measures for satisfying the aspirations. The aim of Abraham Lincoln to become president of the United States was fruitful due to his passionate positive approach towards it, which is the foremost appeal of the notion of the goal. He has set the example of an ideal leader, and his leadership attributes, along with humane practices, have represented the ideology of his ethical behavior for the learners.

Organizational members often follow the behavior of their leader in the workplace, and it is the responsibility of a leader to use the emotional perspective wisely, behave ethically, and perform his role sincerely in the organization. An understanding of the behavior of the group members plays an effective role in defining their tasks (Anbuvelan, 2017), because a well-specified goal is helpful for people to make more progress (Cooper, 2018). Hence, the concept of goal setting comes under the vital obligations of an organization.

Literature Review

Goal sequencing creates a visual goal stairway to the ultimate long-term goal (Hutcherson, 2014). Goals are intangible and complex (Slade, 2013). It is to have a purpose that directs how we think and act (Moskowitz & Grant, 2009). Affective conditions or skills indicates the progress of the goal process. (Smith, 2014). Recognizing and in-corporating reality is vital to effective goal setting (Blair, 2003). Effective goals which have written in specific measurable terms, are achievable, have realistic deadlines, manageable, and analyzed for their potential problems (Dobson & Wilson, 2008). A human organism (an individual) must continuously evaluate and respond to stimuli that either enhance or endanger their ability to survive, and those that develop successful features to accomplish these goals are more likely to pass on their genes. Emotions have evolved as one mechanism to direct the organism towards this purpose (Rathus & Sanderson, 1998). The theory of goal-directed actions recognizes that we process emotionally anchored information at the individual and group levels and suggests that emotions serve to energize individual and group goal setting in actions, projects, and careers (Valach & Wald 2002).

Emotions have been dealt with by philosophers since ancient times (Mohla, 2015). The oldest known classification of emotions has held in the Hellenistic philosophy of stoicism (TenHouten, 2014). Emotions are always the outcome of the balance of multiple appraisals, multiple meanings, and relevance to multiple concerns (Frijda, 2004). Rasas are nispati (having no Knowledge element but for sure have emotive inclinations (Sharma, 2018). Bhavas are often translated as feeling, emotion, or mood, while rasas are the outcome of bhava or created by bhava (Pratishtha, 2015). Rasa is the essence of all that is inside and outside, the feeling nature of both the self and the universe (Marchand, 2006). The context of the goal involves principles of goal setting and goal implementation (Grant & Gelety, 2009). A goal provides organizations with general directions concerning what should happen (Kirst-Ashman, 2007). During the goal-striving phase, a person deals with threats and opportunities arising during goal pursuit and eventually attains the goal (Bagozzi et al., 2003).

An individual's goals are best accomplished with his tact of well managing the emotional knowledge and intelligence (Denham & Burton,

2012). Emotions assist us in evaluating our alternatives and providing the motivation to make a change (Leahy et al., 2011). Altruism has defined as a motivational state with the ultimate goal of increasing another's welfare (Tappolet, 2014). The body, with its cognitive, emotional, and sensorial apparatus, is controlled through a purity mechanism that involves a renunciation of desire and yoga procedures (Bilimoria & Wenta, 2015). A self-regulation perspective to the motivational research tradition on negotiations has pointed out that the effects of the intervention have implicitly improved the process of goal setting (Trötschel & Gollwitzer, 2007). Goal-setting theory is not limited to but focuses primarily on motivation in work settings (Locke & Latham, 2002). Setting demanding goals and persistently acting on them are important prerequisites for successful goal striving (Brandstätter & Frank, 2006). A deliberative mindset channelizes the psychological power to identify the expected values of potential goals (Gollwitzer et al., 2003). The mind-set shows a moment of inertia in individuals because it does not vanish immediately when the task activity is over (Gollwitzer, 2011). There should be a feasible objective and suitable standards to have effective control in the organization (Anbuvelan, 2017). In the process of goal-pursuit, an individual's role behavior depends on means-end premises as well as goal premises (Simon, 1964).

Ancient Indian literature, like the *Puranas, Shastras*, and the inscriptions, has preserved the genealogies of royal dynasties (Sen, 1999). According to the Vedic world view, the world has pervaded by divinity, and every living being aims to achieve liberation (Sharma & Sharma, 1996). Folk tales have ancient roots in Eastern religion, and their applications of the modem version turn the ancient parables moral become fruitful in the contemporary disciplines of learning (Zlotnick, 2001). One of the important benefits of the human mind is that it has programmed with equal efficiency irrespective of age (Menon, 2005). The stories of *Panchatantra* have included the lessons which act as guidance for the wise conduct of life. It has vital importance in the world literature for its contribution in the field of practical wisdom (Kulkarni, 2013). An intellectual leader always evaluates the outcomes of alternative actions in terms of the goal (Griffin & Moorhead, 2011). Goal pursuit is initiated when matches between and one's current state to an undesired state are detected (Fujita & MacGregor, 2012). During the goal process, people experience a positive effect when they appear attainable (Cooper, 2018).

The Ancient Concept of Emotions like *Rasa-Siddhanta* and its Pertinence in Goal setting

The goal content approach has yielded deep insights into the emotional phenomena of passion, despair, success, and well-being (Grant & Gelety, 2009), and an individual's emotional experience has a central role in his practice of goal pursuit (Maglio et al., 2014). An emotion is a neutrally implemented state that operates in a domain-specific manner on the information (Adolphs, 2005), and its vital states have significantly affected the goal process, and to make it fruitful (Plemmons &Weiss, 2013). Emotions guide our thinking in ways that allow us to act sensibly under conditions of uncertainty (Leithwood & Beatty, 2007), and each basic feeling is not a single emotion but, rather, a family of sentiments that revolves around a particular theme, for example, joy includes all emotions related to making progress on a goal theme which includes satisfaction, relief, enthusiasm, contentment, amusement, and pride (Reeve, 2014). The presence of sincere emotions in an individual reflects its genuine character. In the task of determining and executing the goals of an organization, it is vital to analyze the explicit character-force of the appropriate people involved, because the inclusion of emotional intelligence provides strength to the leader in the decision-making process and accordingly, emotions have viewed as the first and foremost kind of judgment (Frijda, 2004). They have acted as a significant component in people's pursuit of goals (Bagozzi et al., 2003).

The Indian context of the emotional intelligence concept has embedded in its highly valued social concerns, virtues, religious traditions, and cultural practices (Behera, 2016). Ancient sages, seers, and yogis deeply understand that mind, body, and spirit are closely related because emotions are those powerful forces that exist simultaneously both in our mind and body (Frawley & Kshirsagar, 2018). According to the Indian philosophy of Ayurveda, our moods and emotions are continuously affected by the play of the elements, senses, and vital energy in our body (Marchand, 2006). The study of aesthetic emotions represents an interdisciplinary region of affective science (Silvia, 2014), and the concept of emotional intelligence in organizational leadership has its basic wisdom from the concept of *Navras* from *Natya Shastra* (200 BCE and 200 CE), which is an epic text written by Bharata Muni (Ahmad, 2015). An aesthetic mood has termed in the *Sanskrit* language as *rasa*, and the ancient treatise on Indian literature of arts has identified nine types of *rasas* (the states of mind) such as *Shringar, Hasya, Karuna, Adhbut, Raudra, Veer, Bhayanaka, Bibhatsya,* and *Shantha* (Nayar, 1989). The difference between recognizing the emotion and experiencing it in real life has summarized by the word Rasa (Dace, 1963).

Gnoli (1956) observes rasa as permanent mental states of emotions, which has based on three distinct phenomena such that cause (kārana), effects (kārya), and concomitant elements (sahacara). The causes are the effects and mental images that produce the state, the effects are the visible reactions caused by the state, and concomitant elements are the accessory mental disturbances accompanying the state. It is an important link within the body and mind that affects our thoughts and emotions (Marchand, 2006). The goal of human life is to develop its highest potential along with prospering the surroundings, for example, the spiritual goal of humans is to attain self-realization, accompanying the milieu of societal development. The aesthetic mood has termed in *Sanskrit* as rasa and categorization of different rasas has given below:

- In the emotional context of *Shringar-rasa* (Fondness), people have a sensitive approach to the environment and thoughtfully considered all the factors involved in organizational goal achievement procedure and their impact on nature.
- In *Hasya-rasa* (Joy), the well-being of all factors has significantly realized through cheerful ideology.
- In the framework of *Adhbhut-rasa* (Wonder), goals have established to obtain some unusual discoveries.
- A leader is full of *Veer-rasa* (Courage) while performing his leadership tasks, and he targets his objectives with the virtue of valor.
- Intellectuals occupied with the emotional state of *Shanti-rasa* (Peace) have worked to establish universal peace and spread the message of harmony in the society.
- Empathetic leaders have the quality of *Karuna-rasa* (Compassion) and make decisions while considering the emotional perspective of implementing any change in the organization.
- The emotion of being *(Raudra)* Passion or rage in the leader helps to control the anti-trade elements and unethical measures in the organization.

- Individuals who are aware of the consequences of any wrong and illegal effort have an understanding of the emotions of *Bhaya* (Fear) and *Vismaya* (Astonishment) in clear terms.

All these aesthetic rasas or emotions have incorporated in the balanced mind of an intellectual leader and responsible for making ethical choices in goal-setting pursuit. This quality of emotional intelligence helps him to set the goals of the organization's development and take care of the interest of people of all categories involved in goal achievement tasks. The wise use of emotions is a kind of control over senses, but there must be an appropriate balance of all these rasas in an individual. It provides a different perspective on human qualities like a strong mind, vision, determination, humor, energy, courage, passion, etc. Accordingly, the *Rasa-paddhati*, which has rooted in the ancient period, is fruitful to identify the mental states and provided a new contemporary approach to explain the emotional framework of individuals.

Emotions affect the process of thinking and understanding of human beings, and they have a comprehensive impact on their behavior. There is reciprocate interchange of expressions during the goal attainment process in the group members, and it requires emotional regulation in the organization. The likelihood of accessing an emotion has increased by presenting information that maximizes the number of propositions matched (Rathus & Sanderson, 1998). Emotions play a central organizing role in an individual's experience of reality, sense of self, and cooperative and competitive orientations towards others (TenHouten, 2014). They have produced when input cues match concept in the network and therefore activate the affected network (Rathus & Sanderson, 1998). The psychology of emotions has preoccupied itself in identifying the role of the emotions in behavior, which have social consequences as well (Frijda, 1996), because emotions are regulators of behavior within ourselves, (intrapersonal), and in interaction with others (interpersonal) (Denham & Burton, 2012). All the emotional states which are experienced by an individual have closely connected with the functioning of the body (Bilimoria & Wenta, 2015). The emotional involvement with the creative outcome operates on both the group as well as an individual level (Laycock, 2005).

The Consequences of Ethical Goals and their Influence in Developing Human Character

The ancient Indian scholar named as Kauṭilya or Vishnugupta or Chanakya (371 BC- 283 BC), has significantly enriched the field of administration or sovereignty through his literary works. The *Arthaśāstra*, composed and written in Sanskrit, is a very valuable guide for monarchs and a rulebook for citizens. It deals with issues concerning diplomatic skills, political economy, and general secular knowledge. It has translated by Dr. Shamasastry of the Mysore Governmental Oriental Library in 1905. Kautilya deals at considerable length with the complexities and duplicities required for a Leader/ King to pursue his relationships with his peers. It contains numerous references to varied issues of social rights for people, and these rights lead to greater incentives for work and productivity in a country. Ancient Indian texts have included the works of multiple authors, and have refined and embellished, long after the core sections had written by the original author. This piece of literature has undertaken with great love and respect for the memory of that original author (Avari, 2016). According to the exposition given in the *Arthaśāstra,* the king who wishes, for a long and prosperous jurisdiction, should follow the rules of conduct that include the control of his senses 'by eliminating vices of desire, anger, greed, pride, arrogance, and excitability' (Bilimoria & Wenta, 2015). This text contains the concepts of economics, politics, ethics, war, and law, and the revolutionary theory of value, which has derived from the utility of the product (Vylder & Mulla, 2014).

Kautilya, the great Indian philosopher, and statesman, in writing his epic treatise on the art of good government has enunciated classified views on international trade, principles of taxation, and the labour theory of value (Waldauer et al., 1996). His theory of public organization emerges from his suggestions about the duties and responsibilities of the king and discussions of various departments and their workforces (Kumar, 2005), and its approach was essentially synthetic as he did not want to destroy old traditions but wanted to give new meaning to them (Chousalkar, 2004). The *Arthaśāstra* is a scholarly treatise that is a kind of an inquiry into the oriental and western literary relations in the literature of political consciousness (Alphonso-Karakala, 1975), and it followed the methodology developed by the different philosophical traditions in ancient India (Chousalkar, 2004). This text has potential applicability and relevance with the corporate strategic planning process in the modern environment (Starzl & Dhir, 1986). Prasoon (2012, p. 39) has emphasized on the Chankaya Sutra or aphorisms in his work regarding ethical human behavior. He writes. 'Humility is the root of sense control'. A phrase or *neeti* of Chankaya defining the significance and dimension of goal perspectives has given here:

Karmaayattam Phalam Pusaam Buddhih Karmaanusaarini.
Tathapi Sudhiyaachaaryaah Suvichaaryava Kurvate.

Although a man intention to always act wisely in a controlled manner, yet an intellectual considerately measures the good or bad outcome of any action (Chaturvedi, 2017). It means that in the process of goal-setting procedure, a leader should carefully evaluate all the effects and consequences of any new plan, practice, and task execution in the organizational environment.

The term goal, which has used in coaching or leadership activity, is far more than the simplistic SMART acronym implies (Grant, 2012). During the process of goal setting, whether at a professional or personal level, a person needs to analyze all the relevant features of the goal like specific, measurable, achievable, realistic, and time-bound while implementing it in the organization, and it shows the cleverness of the people engaged in the task. Smart action planning presented by the leaders exhibits a firm knowledge of the goal's concept and execution of the work cleverly in the organization. The two main attributes of a goal that are responsible for its effectiveness are content and intensity. In the content part, there are three aspects, such as specification, challenge, and conclusion of the target. The intensity part includes the commitment to the target and self-efficacy, which has further linked with motivational actions included in the goal mechanism, such as persistence and appropriate directional approach. Therefore, The SMART framework provides a criterion to a leader for goal setting while considering the feasibility, prospects, and effects of the goals in the organizational environment.

Breathnach (1996) writes that a person accomplishes his desires or wishes only if he actually wants them sincerely or heartily. The love of all mankind is central to the Santana dharma philosophy and the values of Indian life enshrined in the phrases of Vasudhaive Kutumbakam (Mohanty, 2000). The spiritual dimension entails the human proclivity to connect with something greater than oneself, typically involving abstract spiritual divine beings or entities (Kesebir & Pyszczynski, 2012). Thus, an ideal leader who has indulged in the goal-setting process performs the swot analysis of the organization, creates strategic plans for transforming the present conditions, and manages his emotions intelligently at the workplace.

Recognizing the Notion of Goals and Effectiveness of a Positive Mind-Set through Tales

A leader's manner of operating and functioning the organizational tasks indicates his attributes and the kind of mind-set, which also reflects his strength of emotional intelligence. Goal theory prophesies the properties related to the goal, such as level, difficulty, specificity, interaction with individual differences, such as self-efficacy and the need for achievement, to determine a personal level of motivation and performance (Brown et al., 1997). The process of goal setting has based on the average prior performance of those characters that have performed the task and include first a reaction time task and the second an idea-generation task (Locke et al., 1989). Personal control act as strong cognition to being protected from the external environment (Thompson & Schlehofer, 2008). Goals are valuable toward the obligation of work by group members, and they have regarded as essential for future happiness and fulfilment (MacLeod & O'Conner, 2018). Cognitive processes are positively associated with potential goals (Gollwitzer, 2011), and the goal is determined merely by its desirability to the individual, as a function of fantasy, not feasibility (Moskowitz, 2012). An individual role in the organization defines his actions and prospective behavior during diverse circumstances (Simon, 1964). In the goal-setting process, planning, and implementation of chosen goals indices a general cognitive orientation that favors the effective implementation of goals (Gollwitzer & Bayer, 1999).

The narratives serve a meaningful purpose to understand matters of life, and we use stories to organize our experiences and keep ourselves balanced in complex situations (David, 2016). The notion of purpose and its effect on the individual performance has idealized through a tale here:

In a jungle, an old lion was lived along with other animals, and a young stag was also lived there, where the policy of might is the right was working, and weak animals were killed by the mighty animals for food because nature has systematically set the food cycle for them and everyone was indulged in searching and arranging the food for themselves.

One day, a lion was chasing the stag, but he was able to run faster than him and disappeared into the bushes and saved his life, while the stag could run faster than the lion for a shorter period, and the lion could run faster than the stag for a longer period. Other animals who were present there, asked the lion that he could run faster than the stag, so why he let him go?

The lion told them that he was running for saving his life, while I was running merely for a meal. Surely, he could not run faster than me, but he thought that it was the end of his life, while it was a loss of one meal only for me. Hence, the purpose of any act is very important because the performance of a person is mainly depending on the purpose or objective of doing the work (Dadhich, 2012). This story illustrates the kind of individual's purpose, the operation of the activity accordingly, and its effect contained in it. It shows that inclusive determinants of the goal have a crucial role in strategic planning, implementation of executable efforts, and his evolving willingness to achieve the goal. It has a very important lesson in the practice of goal pursuit, whether the purpose is big or small, a leader's perpetual action and determined approach make it possible to realize in the present environment. A person's ethical efforts and wisely decisional works make his life meaningful, like, pearls threaded in a rosary elaborate an embellishment, similarly, his notable purposes, become the jewels of his personality.

The psychology of a positive mind-set has a unique contribution to the process of goal pursuit. Christoff (2018) finds that the framework to deserve the goal includes doing everything needed to reach the goal, taking the required actions, and doing it for as long as it takes. The planning of potential goals facilitates task-relevant cognitive procedures (Gollwitzer, 2011). Cognitive orientations (mind-sets) associated with specific action plans affect goal-directed behavior (Brandstätter & Frank, 2006). A deliberative mind-set involves procedures of measuring advantages and disadvantages, whereas the implemental mind-set involves procedures of scheduling and ordering of goal-oriented actions (Gollwitzer et al., 2003). The deliberative mind-set provides a window to realism, as it can reduce people's pervasive positive illusion, and it serves the accuracy motive when people evaluate themselves while the implemental mind-set enhances people's pervasive positive illusions, and it serves the self-enhancement motive when people evaluate themselves (Gollwitzer & Bayer, 1999).

The brain is a part of the central nervous system, and the frontal lobe is the portion of the brain that manages memory, emotions, hearing, language, and deals with intellectual tasks, decision making, goal-setting, and problem-solving (Namm & Kaufman, 2011). Nayar (1989) states that the mind has to be kept entirely free from any preconceived ideas or theories in the process of developing the goal-setting mechanism. The mind is like a garden if you sow seeds, nurture them with care, and water it daily, you will see a thousand bejeweled red-hued rose-bushes bloom. Thus, if you set goals, nurture them with positive affirmations, water them creative visualization daily, you will see a thousand meaningful coincidences happen, and the law of synchronicity will guide you with their hidden hand, and you will reach your goal unconsciously through little effort (Menon, 2005). Therefore, a leader should have to wisely control his emotions while conducting work-related activities and have respect for the sentiments of his co-workers.

An Interpretation of Significant *Rasas* Required for the Goal Accomplishment

A leader has to traverse various stages and circumstances to achieve the target, which are posed challenges and obstacles during the organizational process. Because working in an organization or a group often creates anomalies among individuals due to emotional and psychological reasons such as dishonor by high authority, lower morale, discouragement of enthusiasm, disparity, depression and painful experiences, non-cooperative behavior, loneliness, wavering attitude, external and internal pressure, fear, depravity, etc., and under organizational functioning, all these diverse and parallel circumstances could be controlled by the insight of strong determination that is initiated by his intrinsic qualities. It has been also observed that a person in a goal-attainment process often deviates from his path despite getting off to a good start with all required resources, management system, and well-developed strategies. The main reason for this is the emotional lack of perseverance and commitment to work as despite having not any distinct opportunities or resources during the goal process, emotional mindfulness works as an amazing power like to find a diamond from coal or to blossom lotus from mud. Therefore, the true spirit as well as strong determination enhances his aptitude, leads him on the path of progress to betterment, and makes him more valuable, powerful, and impeccable. Following the path of goal attainment required a true zeal, commitment, and diligence, which has been illustrated through a story along with a lesson to overcome all these evolved reasons. This is a perspective that represents how the mere emotion of determination is highly beneficial.

In the ancient state of India, a devotee used to worship God by sitting under the old tamarind tree daily. One day a deity has visited him. During their conversation, the devotee asked him that whenever he will go to God, please ask, when he will meet me. After some time, he went to God and asked that when he will meet that person who is sitting under the tamarind tree at that place and chanting his name.

God said that he will meet him after many births equivalent to the number of leaves of that tamarind tree. He got upset by listening to his answer and went to that devotee but did not say anything to him. Then he requested that what the Supreme deity has replied, please say it. He said that his answer was disappointing and explained it after his insistence. The devotee asked curiously whether God himself said so.

After hearing his yes, he danced happily that he will meet him because their words can't be false. Suddenly, God appeared in no time. Both were surprised to see him there and asked how he came so early?

The Supreme deity said that when the deity inquired about it and the speed with which the devotee was doing hymn at that time, it would have taken as many births for him. But now his movement has changed and dancing with fun by positive thinking of definitely meeting me.

Therefore, I have come to bless him, because, in the accomplishment of purpose, there is unwavering faith, exclusivity, perseverance, and enthusiasm, which makes the process of goal achievement more active. His true emotions make this meeting possible despite the delay.

Consequently, it is very important to have genuine feelings in achieving anything (Dhawan, 2014). During the task accomplishment sometimes, a well-organized and confident person also loses hope of achieving the desired target due to a delay in the outcome, but it is the power of a positive attitude and strong determination which make the goal process alive and active. Accordingly, despite all the difficulties, speculations, exercises, and obstacles, it is very important to have a firm belief and determination in the achievement of the set target. Therefore, the sentimental effect of emotions has a crucial role in the goal-setting process of the organization.

Eventually, strong determination, patience, and belief interpret the merit of leadership in real terms which required a constant amalgamation of significant rasas as emotional intelligence or mindfulness. In the organizational business, a leader's dedication to his work implies his fondness, performing the work with pleasure shows his joyful attitude, implementing new strategies in the work defines his versatility, facing the odds on the strength of valor shows his courage, controlling the internal obstructions with a calm mind refers his tranquility, and kind behavior with everyone shows his compassion. The qualitative power of these different emotions gives him mental strength which increases his characterful force as well as enhances the personality. So, for the fruitful operation of the organizational work, coordination of emotion involves the incorporation of various significant rasas like *Shringar-rasa, Hasya-rasa, Adhbhut-rasa, Veer-rasa, Shanti-rasa*, and *Karuna-rasa* which have been identified here:

- *Shringar-rasa* means to have a sense of modification or beautification which shows that the leader has the ability to see magnificence in every task like an artist and he endeavors to make it fine and accurate. He performs his work gracefully but not hurriedly or lethargically. It shows its effective executable planning, which helps him to carry out his daily tasks smoothly and timely. For making the goal process distinct, a leader needs to identify the value of the ordinary work to make it amazing, which occurs with a sense of astonishment through *Adhbhut-rasa*, and this emotional approach is imperative in remodeling the tasks for better results.

- *Hasya-rasa* means to have a sense of happiness and enjoyably performing the work by the leader. It illustrates that the leader

has excellent communication skills, humor, and pleasant personality. His expressions reflect the happy state of mind through
gestures or body language during the conversation, so the work
that has been done with cheerful and enjoyable emotions com-
municatively conveys his excellence. It also shows his amiability
and people can interact with him open-heartedly because his af-
fable nature attracts everyone towards him.

- Fearlessness and valor are essential in every task because an individual's attribute of indomitable courage empowers him to
overcome the condition of despair. Due to the sense of bravery
(*Veer-rasa*), he does not get panic rather faces the situation and
patiently solicits solutions to all problems. His endurance and
strength of courage prove to be effective in making him reach the
heights. Because every organizational goal has a definite result
that can be achieved through executing it with full spirit according to the desired output, and this power also helps to fight all
odds that arise during the work and after its completion.

- Calmness and quiet nature both are intrinsic qualities of an individual, which manifest his strength rather than weakness. Conflicts are usually the part of organizational work but solving all
problems in a peaceful manner, without hurting or troubling an-
yone, definitely showed the immense strength and tolerance
power of a wise leader. Controlling power does not mean to be
overbearing but to resolve the issues and complications with
mindfulness and tranquility. So, the functions of controlling and
directing can work effectively with emotional intelligence from
the organizational perspective which required a sense of peace
(*Shanti-rasa*).

- *Karuna-rasa* means compassion. The accomplishment of an organizational goal is group work that requires coordination as
well as the cooperation of all its members and the required objects. This process demands an attitude of belongingness of the
leader with all the people involved in the task and a sense of their
needs and difficulties. With an emotional outlook of compassion,
he behaves sensitively to the members and also helps them in
nurturing their talent. He does not keep to his interests only but
also takes care of all and be aware of events around him and
manages everything properly.

Hence in the organization functioning, the ancient concept of emotions as *Rasa-Paddhati* or *Rasa-Siddhanta*, and the role of rasas have a significant influence on the effectiveness of the goal-setting process. Like, for getting better output through enhancement and modification in the tasks and strategies, a leader should have the emotions of fondness (*Shringar-rasa*) and wonder (*Adhbhut-rasa*); For proper communication and information exchange, and to make the work enjoyable, he must have the emotion of joy and humor (*Hasya-rasa*); For working courageously during the crisis, he must have the emotion of valour (*Veer-rasa*); For resolving the conflicts and issues peacefully, he must have the emotion of calmness (*Shanti-rasa*).; For maintaining proper coordination among group members and understanding their needs, he must have the emotion of compassion (*Karuna-rasa*). Accordingly, these theoretical expressions are really valuable and applicable to understand the concept of emotions through their ancient form as rasas in organizational working.

The realization of goals helps to develop and refine the personality of an individual by the activities enshrined in its attainment because all the ethical measures, approaches, judgments, practices, and other related aspects, which have applied by an individual in his goal attainment task, represent the vision of an organization and its work efficiency. The intensity of positive emotions has a vital role and effect in the goal-setting process, which confirms the prospect of the objective and an individual's potential to achieve it.

Conclusion

Ideal goals help to improve mindfulness by developing positive thoughts and emotions, which provides a way to succeed and synergize the individual's actions in the right direction. A careful observation of emotional intelligence along with a positive attitude provides the potential and strength to an individual to accomplish the objectives of life because the attainment of the goal entails the inclusion of several related procedures, facts, efforts, persistent approach, and strategies. Stories play an inevitable role in representing goal-oriented practices and their implication, by realizing the necessity of objectives and infuse inspiration within the individual, and useful to understand the true value of life as well as emotions. A purposeful task expresses the meaning of life effectively because the work done with determination and confidence gets acclamation and prospective stimulation from people, and accordingly, the passion or enthusiasm, cognizance or knowledge, and an honest vision of the leader have a fundamental aspect in the commencement of the goal-setting process.

Key Takeaways

- Significant goals play a very specific role to transform and sustain people's lives in the right way.
- The ancient framework of emotions as *Rasa-Siddhanta* has a vital implication to understand the emotional psychology of organizational leaders and their behavior in the goal process.
- An ethical purpose helps introduce an individual to his excellence and potential by examining his qualities, uprightly, and drives his inner spirit.
- Maintaining a positive attitude during goal attainment functions as an effective force of working with enthusiasm.
- *Rasas* have influential psychological power which enables a leader to work with a firm belief and strong determination, during the goal-setting process.

Reflection Questions

- How goals are helpful to execute the organizational functioning and provide the right direction for employees to fulfil their interests?
- What is the ancient *Rasa-Paddhati*, and its specificity to understand the emotional framework in today's context?
- How does an appropriate and ethical objective develop the character of humans and enrich their life?
- Why does a leader need to have a positive mind-set for the goal-setting process and its achievement?
- How the psychological coordination of the *rasas* provides emotional strength to a person to become determined towards objectives?

Notes

1. The goal has a valuable function in the organizational environment, and a well-organized goal-setting mechanism and practices involved in its achievement have a vital aspect in the overall effectiveness and productivity of the organization (Gamage, 2006; Griffin & Moorhead, 2011; Jain et al., 1997; Locke & Latham, 2002).

2. A person's ability of emotional control works as a strong force in his task of goal-achievement (Frijda, 2004; Leithwood & Beatty, 2007; Rathus & Sanderson, 1998)/

3. The concept of emotions has theorized as *Rasas* in the ancient Indian literature, which is relevant in the contemporary world and presents an important perspective of understanding the emotions (Dace, 1963; Gnoli, 1956; Nayar, 1989; Marchand, 2006).

4. The practice of goal setting must include a brainstorming approach to its prospects, effects, and consequences, and the treatise based on principles and ethics, like the *Arthaśāstra*, has contained the significant guidelines for human conduct (Breathnach, 1996; Bilimoria & Wenta, 2015; Chaturvedi, 2017, Prasoon, 2012, p. 39; Waldauer et al., 1996).

5. Acumen introduces a rational mind that reflects a leader's strong mindset, positive thinking, and skill of intellectual actions. Tales or narratives based on mindfulness are useful in learning the importance of set targets, which represents their applicability in understanding the human attributes (Gollwitzer & Bayer, 1999; Gollwitzer et al., 2003; Christoff, 2018; Locke et al., 1989; Thompson & Schlehofer, 2008).

References

Adolphs, R. (2005). 'Could a Robot have Emotions? Theatrical Perspectives from Social Cognitive Neuroscience'. In Fellous, J-M. and Arbib, M. A. (Eds), Who Needs Emotions? *The Brain Meets the Robot.* Oxford, United Kingdom: Oxford University Press, 9-28.

Agarwal, R. (1982). *Organization and Management.* New Delhi, India: Tata McGraw-Hill Education.

Ahmad, A. (2015). 'Foreword'. In Mohla, N., *Human Drama Inc.: Emotional Intelligence in the Workplace.* New Delhi, India: SAGE Publications India, vii-x.

Alphonso-Karakala, J. B. (1975). 'Facets of Panchatantra'. *Indian Literature, Sahitya Akademi,* **18**, 73-91.

Anbuvelan, K. (2017). *Principles of Management.* New Delhi, India: Firewall Media.

Avari, B. (2016). *India: The Ancient Past: A History of the Indian Subcontinent from c. 7000 BCE to CE 1200.* Abingdon, United Kingdom: Routledge.

Bagozzi, R. P., Baumgartner, H., Pieters, R., & Zeelenberg, M. (2003). 'The Role of Emotions in Goal-Directed Behaviour'. In Huffman, C., Mick, D. G. and Ratneshwar, S. (Eds), *The Why of Consumption: Contemporary Perspectives on Consumer Motives, Goals and Desires.* Abingdon, United Kingdom: Routledge, 36-58.

Barlow, D. H., Ellard, K. K., Fairholme, C. P., Farchione, T. J., Boisseau, C. L., May, J. E. T., & Allen, L. B. (2010). *Unified Protocol for Transdiagnostic Treatment of Emotional Disorders: Workbook.* Oxford, United Kingdom: Oxford University Press.

Behera, A. K. (2016). 'Understanding Emotional Intelligence in Educational Context'. *International Journal of Humanities and Social Science Invention,* **5**, 17-28.

Berger, F., & Brownwell, J. (2012). *Organizational Behaviour for the Hospitality Industry.* Chennai, India: Pearson Education India.

Bilimoria, P., & Wenta, A. (2015). 'Emotions in Indian Though-Systems: An Introduction'. In Bilimoria, P. and Wenta, A. (Eds), *Emotions in Indian Thought-Systems.* Abingdon, United Kingdom: Routledge, 1-56.

Blair, G. R. (2003). *Goal Setting for Results: Success Strategies for You and Your Organization.* Texas, United States: The Walk The Talk Company.

Brandstätter, V., & Frank, E. (2006). 'The Role of Implemental Verses Deliberative Mindsets in Goal-Setting and Goal-Directed Persistence'. In Frey, D., Mandl, H. and Rosenstiel, L.V. (Eds), *Knowledge and Action.* Boston, United States: Hogrefe Publishing, 7-22.

Breathnach, S. B. (1996). *The Simple Abundance Journal of Gratitude.* Sydney, Australia: Hachette.

Brophy, J. (2008). 'Scaffolding Appreciation for School Learning: An Update'. In Maehr, M. L., Karabenick, S. A. and Urdan, T. C. (Eds), *Social Psychological Perspectives.* Bingley, United Kingdom: Emerald Group Publishing, 1-48.

Brown, S. P., Cron, W. L., & Slocum, J. W. (1997). 'Effects of Goal-Directed Emotions on Salesperson Volitions, Behaviour, and Performance: A Longitudinal Study'. *Journal of Marketing, 61*, 39-50.

Cavallo, J. V., & Fitzsimons, G. M. (2012). 'Goal Competition, Conflict, Coordination, and Completion: How Inter-goal Dynamics Affect Self-Regulation'. In Aarts, H. and Elliot, A. J. (Eds), *Goal-directed Behaviour.* London, United Kingdom: Psychology Press, 267-300.

Chaturvedi, B. K. (2017). 'Consequence of an Action'. *Chanakya Neeti.* New Delhi, India: Diamond Pocket Books (P) Ltd.

Chousalkar, A. S. (2004). 'Methodology of Kautilya's Arthashastra'. *The Indian Journal of Political Science, 65*, 55-76.

Christoff, C. (2018). *Goal Setting For People Who Can't Set Goals: Proven Tools and Techniques to Achieve Anything You Want.* Victoria, Australia: Global Publishing Group.

Cooper, M. (2018). 'The Psychology of Goals: A Practice-Friendly Review'. In Cooper, M. and Law, D. (Eds), *Working with Goals in Psychotherapy and Counselling.* Oxford, United Kingdom: Oxford University Press, 35–71.

Dace, W. (1963). 'The Concept of "Rasa" in Sanskrit Dramatic Theory'. *Educational Theatre Journal,* The Johns Hopkins University Press, **15**, 249-254.

Dadhich, C. L. (2012). 'Lion & Stag'. *Management through Folk Wisdom.* New Delhi, India: Diamond Books.

Daniels, N. (2013). *Goal Planning Strategies That Truly Work: How To Reach Any Goal You Wish.* Munich, Germany: BookRix GmbH & Co. KG.

David, S. (2016). *Emotional Agility: Get Unstuck, Embrace Change and Thrive in Work and Life.* London, United Kingdom: Penguin UK.

Denham, S. A., & Burton, R. (2012). *Social and Emotional Prevention and Intervention Programming for Pre-Schoolers.* Berlin, Germany: Springer Science & Business Media.

Dhawan, R. (2014). *Dridh Uddeshya Se Labh. Aadarsh Kahaniya.* Gorakhpur, India: GitaPress.

Dobson, M., & Wilson, S. B. (2008). *Goal Setting: How to Create an Action Plan and Achieve Your Goals.* New York, United States: AMACOM.

Frawley, D., & Kshirsagar, S. (2018). *Art and Science of Vedic Counselling.* New Delhi, India: Lotus Press.

Frijda, N. H. (1996). 'Passions: Emotion and Socially Consequential Behaviour'. In Kavanaugh,R. D., Zimmerberg, B. and Fein, S. (Eds), *Emotion: Interdisciplinary Perspectives.* London, United Kingdom: Psychology Press, 1-28.

Frijda, N. H. (2004). 'Emotions and Action'. In Manstead, A. S. R., Frijda, N. and Fischer, A. (Eds), *Feelings and Emotions: The Amsterdam Symposium.* Cambridge, United Kingdom: Cambridge University Press, 158-173.

Fujita, K., & MacGregor, K. E. (2012). 'Basic Goal Distinctions'. In Aarts, H. and Elliot, A. J. (Eds), *Goal-directed Behaviour.* London, United Kingdom: Psychology Press, 85-114.

Gamage, D. (2006). *Professional Development for Leaders and Managers of Self-Governing Schools.* Berlin, Germany: Springer Science & Business Media.

Gnoli, R. (1956). 'Introduction'. In Gnoli, R. (Ed.), *The Aesthetic Experience According To Abhinavagupta.* Rome, Italy: Is. M.E.O. [i.e. Istituto italiano per il medio ed Estremo Oriente], xiv-lii.

Gollwitzer, P. M., & Bayer, U. (1999). 'Deliberative Verse Implemental Mind-Sets in the Control of Action'. In Chaiken,S. and Trope, Y. (Eds), *Dual-process Theories in Social Psychology.* New York, United States: Guilford Press, 403-422.

Gollwitzer, P. M., Heckhausen, H., & Steller, B. (2003). 'Deliberative and Implemental Mind-Sets: Cognitive Tuning Toward Congruous Thoughts and Information'. In Arie W. Kruglanski, A.W. and Higgins, E. T. (Eds), *Social Psychology: A General Reader.* London, United Kingdom: Psychology Press, 223-236.

Gollwitzer, P. M. (2011). 'Mind Set theory of Action Phases'. In Lange, P. A. M. V., Kruglanski, A.W. and Higgins, E. T. (Eds), *Handbook of Theories of Social Psychology: Volume One.* California, United States: SAGE, 526-546.

Grant, H., & Gelety, L. (2009). 'Goal Content Theories Why Differences In What We Are Striving For Matter'. In Moskowitz, G. B. and Grant, H. (Eds), *The Psychology of Goals.* New York, United States: Guilford Press, 77-97.

Grant, A. M. (2012). 'An Integrated Model of Goal-focused Coaching: An Evidence-Based Framework for Teaching and Practice'. *International Coaching Psychology Review,* **7**, 146-165.

Griffin, R. W., & Moorhead, G. (2011). *Organizational Behaviour.* Massachusetts, United States: Cengage Learning.

Huffman, C. (2003). *The Why of Consumption: Contemporary Perspec-*

tives on Consumer Motives, Goals and Desires. Abingdon, United Kingdom: Routledge.

Hutcherson, R. (2014). *Organizational Optimization.* Indiana, United States: Author House.

Jain, R. K., Jain, R., & Triandis, H. C. (1997). *Management of Research and Development Organizations: Managing the Unmanageable.* New Jersey, United States: John Wiley & Sons.

Kesebir, P., & Pyszczynski, T. (2012). 'The Role of Death in Life: Existential Aspects of Human Motivation'. In Ryan, R. M. (Ed.), *The Oxford Handbook of Human Motivation.* New York, United States: Oxford University Press, USA, 43-64.

Kirst-Ashman, K. (2007). *Human Behaviour, Communities, Organizations, and Groups in the Macro Social Environment: An Empowerment Approach.* Massachusetts, United States: Cengage Learning.

Kulkarni, S. (2013). 'Panchatantra – An Example of Using Narratives in Teaching in Ancient Indian Education'. Teoksessa Eero Ropo & Maiju Huttunen (toim.) Tampere: Tampere University Press, 199–216.

Kumar, A. (2005). 'The Structure and Principles of Public Organization in Kautilya's Arthashastra'. *The Indian Journal of Political Science,* **66**, 463-488.

Latham, G. P. (1991). 'Self-Regulation through Goal Setting'. *Organizational Behaviour and Human Decision Processes,* 212-247.

Laycock, J. (2005). *A Changing Role for the Composer in Society: A Study of the Historical Background and Current Methodologies of Creative Music-making.* Bern, Switzerland: Peter Lang.

Leahy, R. L., Tirch, D. D., & Napolitano, L. A. (2011). *Emotion Regulation in Psychotherapy: A Practitioner's Guide.* New York, United States: Guilford Press.

Leithwood, K., & Beatty, B. (2007). 'Teacher Emotions, School Reform, and Student Learning: A Leadership Perspective'. In Leithwood, K.

and Beatty, B. (Eds), *Leading With Teacher Emotions in Mind.* California, United States: Corwin Press, 1-12.

Locke, E. A., Chah, D. O., Harrison, S., & Lustgarten, N. (1989). 'Separating the Effects of Goal Specificity from Goal Level'. *Organizational Behaviour and Human Decision Processes,* **43**, 270–287

Locke, E. A., & Latham, G. P. (2002). 'Building a Practically Useful Theory of Goal Setting and Task Motivation-A 35-Year Odyssey'. *American Psychologist,* **57**, 705–717.

Locke, E. A., & Latham, G. P. (2006). 'New Directions in Goal-Setting Theory'. *Current Directions in Psychological Science,* **15**, 265-268.

MacLeod, A. K., & O'Conner, R. C. (2018).' Positive Future Thinking, Well-being and Mental Health'. In Oettingen, G., Sevincer, A. T. and Gollwitzer, P. M. (Eds), *The Psychology Of Thinking About The Future.* New York, United States: Guilford Publications. 199-213.

Maglio, S. J., Gollwitzer, P. M., & Oettingen, G. (2014). Emotion and Control in the Planning of Goals. *Motivation and Emotion Springer,* **38**, 620–634.

Marchand, P. (2006). *The Yoga of the Nine Emotions: The Tantric Practice of Rasa Sadhana.* New York, United States: Simon and Schuster.

Menon, M. (2005). *ZeNLP: The Power to Succeed.* New Delhi, India: SAGE.

Mohanty, J. (2000). 'Democracy and Education: A Plea for Human Rights Education'. In Mohanty, J. (Ed.), *Human Rights Education.* Delhi, India: Deep and Deep Publications, 29-40.

Mohla, N. (2015). *Human Drama Inc.: Emotional Intelligence in the Workplace.* New Delhi, India: SAGE Publications India.

Moskowitz, G. B., & Grant, H. (2009). 'Introduction- Four themes in the Study of Goals'. In Moskowitz, G. B. and Grant, H. (Eds), *The Psychology of Goals.* New York, United States: Guilford Press, 1-26.

Moskowitz, G. B. (2012). The Representation and Regulation of Goals.

In Arts, H. and Elliot, A. J. (Eds), *Goal-directed Behaviour*. London, United Kingdom: Psychology Press, 1-48.

Murphy, M. (2010). *Hard Goals: The Secret to Getting from Where You Are to Where You Want to Be*. New York, United States: McGraw Hill Professional.

Namm, E., & Kaufman, R. (2011). *Change to a Positive Mind set and Extend Your Lifeline: A Journey to Miles of Smiles, Positive Energy Power, Hope, Health and Happiness*. Indiana, United States: Author House.

Nayar, S. (1989). *Bhatkhande's Contribution to Music: A Historical Perspective*. Mumbai, India: Popular Prakashan.

Plemmons, S. A., & Weiss, H. M. (2013). 'Goal and Affect' In Locke, E. A. and Latham G. P. (Eds), *New Developments in Goal Setting and Task Performance*. Abingdon, United Kingdom: Routledge, 117-132.

Pratishtha, A. (2015). *Let's Learn Kathak - I*. Saharanpur, India: Mokshayatan Yog Sansthan.

Prasoon, S. (2012). *Chankaya Sutra. Chanakya: Rules of Governance by the Guru of Governance*. New Delhi, India.

Rathus, J. H., & Sanderson, W. C. (1998). The Role of Emotions in the Psychopathology and Treatment of the Anxiety Disorders. In Flack, W. F. and Laird, J. D. (Eds), *Emotions in Psychopathology: Theory and Research*. Oxford, United Kingdom: Oxford University Press, 254-264.

Reeve, J. (2014). *Understanding Motivation and Emotion*. New Jersey, United States: John Wiley & Sons.

Reiss, K. J. (2012). *Be a Change Master: 12 Coaching Strategies for Leading Professional and Personal Change*. California, United States: Corwin Press.

Rohn, J. (2011). 'Nine Thing More Important Than Capital For Achieving Network Marketing Success'. In Rubino, J. (Ed.), *The Ultimate Guide to Network Marketing: 37 Top Network Marketing Income-Earners Share Their Most Preciously Guarded Secrets to Building Extreme*

Wealth. New Jersey, United States: John Wiley & Sons, 17-20.

Schnelle, W. (2008). *A Discursive Approach to Organizational and Strategy Consulting. Norderstedt,* Germany: BoD – Books on Demand.

Sen, S. N. (1999). *Ancient Indian History and Civilization.* New Delhi, India: New Age International.

Shapiro, S. M. (2010). *Goal-Free Living: How to Have the Life You Want NOW!* New Jersey, United States: John Wiley & Sons.

Sharma, R. N., & Sharma, R. K. (1996). *History of Education in India.* New Delhi, India: Atlantic Publishers & Dist.

Sharma, S. (2018). *Translation Studies and Principles of Translation.* Shimla, India: HP University, India.

Silvia, P. J. (2014). 'Aesthetic Emotions (Psychological Perspective)'. In Sander, D. and Scherer, K. (Eds), *Oxford Companion to Emotion and the Affective Sciences.* Oxford, United Kingdom: OUP Oxford, 4-9.

Simon, H. A. (1964). 'On the Concept of Organizational Goal'. *Administrative Science Quarterly,* Vol. 9, No. 1, 1-22.

Slade, S. (2013). *Goal-based Decision Making: An Interpersonal Model.* London, United Kingdom: Psychology Press.

Smith, A. (2014). 'Introduction and Overview'. In Kiresuk, T. J., Smith, A. and Cardillo, J. E. (Eds), *Goal Attainment Scaling: Applications, Theory, and Measurement.* London, United Kingdom: Psychology Press, 1-14.

Starzl, T. W., & Dhir, K. S. (1986). 'Strategic Planning 2300 Years Ago: The Strategy of Kautilya'. *Management International Review,* **26**, 70-77.

TenHouten, W. D. (2014). *Emotion and Reason: Mind, Brain, and the Social Domains of Work and Love.* Abingdon, United Kingdom: Routledge.

Thompson, S., & Schlehofer, M. M. (2008). 'The Many Sides of Control

Motivation: Motives for High, Low and, Illusory Control'. In Shah, J. Y. and Gardner, W. L. (Eds), *Handbook of Motivation Science.* New York, United States: Guilford Press, 41-56.

Trötschel, R., & Gollwitzer, P. M. (2007). 'Implementation Intentions and the Willful Pursuit of Prosocial Goals in Negotiations'. *Journal of Experimental Social Psychology,* **43**, 579–598.

Valach, L., & Wald, J. (2002). 'Action Theoretical Perspective in Rehabilitation'. In Ladislav Valach, L., Young, R. A. and Lynam, M. J. (Eds), *Action Theory: A Primer for Applied Research in the Social Sciences.* Connecticut, United States: Greenwood Publishing Group, 173-198.

Vaswani, J. P. (2015). 'He had fixed his Goals'. *100 Stories You will Never Forget.* Mumbai, India: Jaico Publishing House.

Vylder, G. D., & Mulla, J. (2014). 'Kautilya versus Thiruvalluvar. Inspiration from Indian Ancient Classics for Ethics in Governance and Management'. *Globalization for the Common Good Initiative Journal (GCGI Journal),* **10**, 1-16.

Waldauer, C., Zahka, W. J., & Pal, S. (1996). 'Kautilya's Arthashastra: A Neglected Precursor to Classical Economics'. *Indian Economic Review,* **XXXI**, 101-108.

Zammuto, R. F. (1982). *Assessing Organizational Effectiveness: Systems Change, Adaptation, and Strategy.* New York, United States: SUNY Press.

Zlotnick, D. M. (2001). 'The Buddha's Parable and Legal Rhetoric'. *Washington and Lee Law Review,* **58**, 957-1016.

www.ingramcontent.com/pod-product-compliance
Lightning Source LLC
Chambersburg PA
CBHW071752050426
42335CB00065B/1789